# THE REVOLUTIONISTS

A COMEDY
A QUARTET
A REVOLUTIONARY DREAM FUGUE
A TRUE STORY

BY
LAUREN GUNDERSON

★

★

DRAMATISTS
PLAY SERVICE
INC.

**NOTE ON BILLING**

Anyone receiving permission to produce THE REVOLUTIONISTS is required to give credit to the Author as sole and exclusive Author of the Play on the title page of all programs distributed in connection with performances of the Play and in all instances in which the title of the Play appears, including printed or digital materials for advertising, publicizing or otherwise exploiting the Play and/or a production thereof. Please see your production license for font size and typeface requirements.

Be advised that there may be additional credits required in all programs and promotional material. Such language will be listed under the "Additional Billing" section of production licenses. It is the licensee's responsibility to ensure any and all required billing is included in the requisite places, per the terms of the license.

**SPECIAL NOTE ON "OUR SONG"**

Music for the song used in the play is required for production. There is no royalty fee for the use of this music. Theaters MUST use the approved music; you may not make up or alter the music in any way. A pdf of sheet music can be downloaded at: http://www.dramatists.com/sheetmusic/TheRevolutionistssheetmusic.pdf

THE REVOLUTIONISTS was commissioned and first produced by the Cincinnati Playhouse in the Park (Blake Robison, Artistic Director; Buzz Ward, Managing Director) in February, 2016. It was directed by Eleanor Holdridge, the scenic and costume designs were by Marion Williams, the lighting design was by Mark Barton, the sound design was by Scott Killian, and the stage manager was Andrea L. Shell. The cast was as follows:

OLYMPE DE GOUGES ................................................ Lise Bruneau
CHARLOTTE CORDAY ............................................... Keira Keeley
MARIE-ANTOINETTE .................................. Jessica Lynn Carroll
MARIANNE ANGELLE ......................................... Kenita R. Miller

## CHARACTERS

OLYMPE DE GOUGES—38. Badass activist playwright and feminist. Theatre nerd, excitable, passionate, a showman. Widowed and never remarried to ensure her personal freedom.

CHARLOTTE CORDAY— 25. Badass country girl and assassin. Very serious, hardened by righteousness, never been kissed. Has a pocket watch she keeps checking. Also plays FRATERNITÉ in a mask.

MARIE-ANTOINETTE—38. Less badass but fascinating former queen of France. Bubbly, graceful, opinionated, totally unaware, unintentionally rude, and oddly prescient. Never had a real friend. Also plays FRATERNITÉ in a mask.

MARIANNE ANGELLE— 30s. A badass black woman in Paris. She is from the Caribbean, a free woman, a spy working with her husband, Vincent. Tough, classy, vigilant, the sanest one of them all.

## SETTING

Paris, the Reign of Terror (1793).
A safe place, a study, a prison cell, the Tribunal.
Then the scaffold.

## PUNCTUATION AS RHYTHM PRIMER

(—) Dashes at the end of a sentence are cut-offs by the following line.

(—) Dashes within a sentence are self cut-offs, an acceleration into the next thought.

(…) Ellipses at the end of a sentence are trail-offs, unsure of what's next.

*(Breath.)* is a small, personal pause.

*(Pause.)* is a shared pause of average duration.

*(Beat.)* is a longer pause in which a personal change or revelation happens.

## LEVELS OF INTENSITY INDICATED BY DIALOGUE FONT

*Italics are more intense than not.*
ALL CAPS ARE VERY INTENSE.
*ALL CAPS AND ITALICS ARE THE MOST INTENSE.*

## NOTES ON THE PLAY

The play is mostly *a comedy.*

The play is based on real women, real transcripts, and real executions.

But remember it's *a comedy.*

The play runs with a seamlessness that necessitates less-realistic sets.

FRATERNITÉ is an almost commedia presence, a stock character of a bad guy, masked.

*In the end, the entire play is in Olympe's mind as she walks up the stairs, onto the scaffold, and to her death.*

# THE REVOLUTIONISTS

## ACT ONE

### PROLOGUE.

*In the dark.*

*A time of unrest in Paris—crisis—danger—threat.*

*The hum of "Our Song" faintly wafts in.*

*The sound of a scared breath that we are breathing.*
*It's our breath—we are trying to steady our breath*
*Breath*
*Breath—*

*Then a sharp white light on, or the engorging shadow of…*
*A guillotine, its blade rising to the top.*

*A gasp.*

*Which slams into:*

### ONE.

*Olympe standing at her writing,*
*startled into an idea for a new play…*

OLYMPE. Well *that's* not a way to start a comedy.
With an execution? That's just basic dramatic writing: Don't start with beheadings. Audiences don't want plays about terror and death—no—they want…hope. Yes, I have to write about…grace and power

in the face of crisis. Artistic defiance. Yes. That's good. There we go.

*Spitballing now, testing out ideas as they come.*

OK, what if I write a play that is the voice of this revolution, but not the hyperbolic, angry-yelling kind. I will write the wise and witty kind that satirizes and inspires and says to the held breath of a rapt audience…"something…profound."
So yeah. We're gonna have to cut the guillotine.

*Marianne has entered with a bag—luggage.*
*She wears a red protest sash that reads: "Revolution for all!"*

MARIANNE. Cut that thing! Serves it right.

OLYMPE. Oh my god, Marianne!

MARIANNE. I know this is crazy to just show up like this but hello and surprise!

*Hugs!*

OLYMPE. Hello and surprise! Oh my god, for a second I thought you were the national guard.

MARIANNE. Are they coming for the writers already?

OLYMPE. Only the important ones. I should be fine. Come in, come in. What are you doing here?

MARIANNE. Many things including, I hope, staying with you. Is that OK?

OLYMPE. Of course! Oh my god. Stay as long as you need.

MARIANNE. Thank you thank you.

OLYMPE. Don't thank me. I'm so glad to see you. I thought you went back to the Caribbean.

MARIANNE. Vincent went back, I stayed in Nice.

OLYMPE. Ooh Nice is nice.

MARIANNE. For some. For me? A lot less beach and a lot more political reconnaissance.

OLYMPE. What does that mean?

MARIANNE. Gathering intelligence to send home. That's why I'm back. Things are heating up and we need an eye in Paris and I'm it.

OLYMPE. So wait. I've been restarting the same play for a month while you became a damn spy?!

MARIANNE. I mean…

OLYMPE. GIRL.

MARIANNE. I know.

OLYMPE. Look at you!

MARIANNE. Well, we decided we needed our own intel, really tap into the political machines or we'll never figure how to break them.

OLYMPE. You are my spy friend! God, you make me so much more interesting.

MARIANNE. Well don't get comfortable, I'm also here because I need you.

OLYMPE. Playwrights *love* hearing that. It's so rare.

MARIANNE. I need you to write for us. Pamphlets, articles, treatises about slavery—

OLYMPE. Monologues?

MARIANNE. Abolition human interest stories.

OLYMPE. But *as* monologues?

MARIANNE. Just—sure. Help us! You're the best writer I know.

OLYMPE. How many do you know?

MARIANNE. *(Lying.) So* many. *(Not lying.)* And you can help people understand what we're fighting for, freedom, justice, humanity, come on.

OLYMPE. Of course I'll help! But why don't *you* write this?

MARIANNE. Because I'm a better spy than I am a writer. Please.

OLYMPE. Yes. I'll write anything you want…as soon as I write my play.

MARIANNE. The play you can't even start? I'm rebelling against slavery and you're battling writer's block.

OLYMPE. *I'm not blocked.* I'm just…mentally…hibernating. There's a lot of pressure to write something profound these days. And then I keep thinking if I come up with a good title it'll get me started. Something tantalizing but really vague like…"*The Revolutionists*."

MARIANNE. You could do better.

OLYMPE. I know. Nothing's working. There is drama everywhere you look these days, why can't I write any of it?!

MARIANNE. You can! Pamphlets! For me! Write the truth that needs writing.

OLYMPE. But that's *your* truth. Which I will totally write, I will, but I also really need something of my own. I need a play that's good and important and annoyingly prescient.

MARIANNE. Then write the truth of an artist staring down a civil war.

OLYMPE. And end up with a play about a playwright writing a play? I'd rather watch a guillotine.

MARIANNE. So would everyone.

OLYMPE. Would they? Dammit. Back to guillotines.

MARIANNE. That's not what I meant.

OLYMPE. Setting: Now. Paris, France, 1793. Guillotines are very big these days. Actually they just came out with small ones too, for kids to kill mice and for wives to make salad.

MARIANNE. That's so messed up.

OLYMPE. It is. Everything is. Which is why the people's revolution has risen up with force enough to remove the king from power—

MARIANNE. and from his own head.

OLYMPE. Exactly. Danger, unrest. An epic battle for freedom and peace—

MARIANNE. For white men.

OLYMPE. Exactly. Which is why *my* play… *(A great idea.)* could be about *women* showing the boys how revolutions are done. Yes! Fighting for their rights to life, liberty, and…divorce.

MARIANNE. Divorce and decapitation?
*(Slipping into couplets.)* I hope it's better than it sounds.

OLYMPE. It's comical yet quite profound

MARIANNE. Just doesn't sound like comedy—

OLYMPE. I know, but that's what it could be.

MARIANNE. You know it's always in the timing,

OLYMPE. Are you hearing all this rhyming?

*Gasp.*

*Maybe I'm writing a musical!*

MARIANNE. Oh god, no one wants a musical about the French Revolution.

OLYMPE. Probably right. How about a solemn, bracing political exposé—

MARIANNE. You're losing me.

OLYMPE. How about a thrilling, hilarious political exposé that will gather us as one community, to be inspired by great French art and—

MARIANNE. To boo at whichever new play they want.

OLYMPE. *They did not boo my play.* The abolition one from last year? No. That sound was the natural cathartic release from years of repressed racism and misogyny.

MARIANNE. So you're writing fantasy now?

OLYMPE. The people leapt to their feet.

MARIANNE. And to the exit.

OLYMPE. To tell their friends.

MARIANNE. That it was…"interesting."

OLYMPE. My plays piss off just the right kind of people thank you very much. Excuse me for trying to do something revolutionary during this revolution. This is our time to make a better world for everyone…who sees my plays.

MARIANNE. You're always so close to selflessness.

OLYMPE. Thank you. See now you've got me thinking. What about a passionate sociopolitical comedy about women's rights and—

MARIANNE. A feminist comedy? Girl, *don't.*

OLYMPE. OK, what if my play *starts out* as a comedy, but it'll *end* as a drama. That's fresh, right? We don't even have a word for that but—

MARIANNE. Like… "Life"?

OLYMPE. Just go with me on this: At first the play is witty and fun, maybe some puppets.

MARIANNE. *Why do you always add puppets.*

OLYMPE. Because!

MARIANNE. You might as well go back to the musical.

OLYMPE. *OK* I'm trying to do something important here.

MARIANNE. Which is maybe why it's sucking so bad.

OLYMPE. *Sometimes conviction sucks.*

MARIANNE. I'm just saying that nobody wants to be *told* what to feel.

OLYMPE. I'm not *telling* them what to feel, I'm *forcing* them.

MARIANNE. That's what pamphlets do! Look. Most people don't have time for the grand dramas, it's the intimate ones that matter. So write your political theatre but remember that for most people it's not about being righteous, it's about being real. So find the heart. Not the...art.

OLYMPE. Why are you better at this than me? I've been trying to come up with a cute couplet like that for days, but I keep dreaming of guillotines and resorting to puppets. I have to write something! This is a revolution! Everyone is making history without me!

MARIANNE. Listen—

OLYMPE. I can't listen when I'm whining.

MARIANNE. You're just blocked. Writers get blocked. It's not a tragedy. Being ripped from your country, stuffed in the belly of a ship, carted across the world, and forced to break your back to make sugar for French pastries is a tragedy. The French are fighting a revolution for *freedom* while running a *slave colony* in the West. That's why I need you writing pamphlets so we can expose the immoral and hypocritical actions that—

OLYMPE. *Oh my god I can write about you!*

MARIANNE. —was not the point I was going for.

OLYMPE. Yes! You're gorgeous, and empowered, and seem to have a very clear character motivation.

MARIANNE. We're not gonna stay friends if you write a play about me.

OLYMPE. *(Narrator voice.)* Marianne Angelle: Activist for freedom from slavery in the Caribbean, lover of cheeses and universal human rights, strong yet sardonically sympathetic.

MARIANNE. *No*, she said, sardonically. *Pamphlets.*

OLYMPE. I am! I will! It will be great research for the play. What you're doing is bold and important. You're a goddamn spy for freedom! That's box office gold! Come on. You make me believe that a better world is possible. If people listen to you. And a lot of me.

MARIANNE. OK they say write what you know, right? But what if you write what you *want*. That's what we're really fighting for isn't it? Women's agency over their own lives.

OLYMPE. Yes.

MARIANNE. The abolition of slavery across the planet.

OLYMPE. *Yes.*

MARIANNE. Maybe you don't need to dress your ideas in drama. You can write a monologue? Why don't you write a manifesto.

OLYMPE. Or…a declaration?

MARIANNE. Sure, yeah. Like the Americans.

OLYMPE. Like the Americans! "We hold these truths and-the-fact-that-women-are-people to be self-evident."

MARIANNE. That sounds pretty revolutionary to me.
Also no risk of puppets. Everybody wins.

*Pause. Olympe likes this. Then she thinks. Seriously.*

OLYMPE. Marianne. Do you dream of guillotines? Every night?

MARIANNE. No. Chains.

*KNOCK KNOCK KNOCK on the door.*

*Olympe and Marianne freeze. Oh no. Then…*

*Knockknockknockknockknock—like a hummingbird knocking, fast and fluttery.*

*Marianne gets on one side of the door with a book held as a weapon if needed, through the door…*

OLYMPE. Who's there?

CHARLOTTE. Who's…*there*?

OLYMPE. Well. *You're* the one at the door, who are you?

CHARLOTTE. You're obviously at the door too, and I'm here for a writer.

MARIANNE. Did she say a writer?

OLYMPE. I think that's what she said.

*Charlotte bursts in with a book.*

CHARLOTTE. YES IT'S WHAT I SAID, I SAID A WRITER, I NEED A WRITER, WHO IS THE WRITER AND WHAT'S MY LINE? Are you a writer? If not— *(Turning to Marianne.)* are *you* a writer? This isn't a complicated question. *Where do they keep the writers, I need a line.*

OLYMPE. I'm sorry, you need a *line*?

CHARLOTTE. That's what I said, but I don't care what *I'd* say, I wanna know what *you'd* say. Isn't that how this works? I need that to be how this works.

MARIANNE. And I need you to back the France off. What do you want? Who sent you?

CHARLOTTE. *I* sent me and, I want some dialogue. That's what you do right? You're that real live lady writer guy? You write plays and stuff.

MARIANNE. And pamphlets about the rights of Caribbean slaves, which means she's very busy and we have no idea who you are or whose side you're on, also you're very loud and immediately unsettling, so why don't we do this another time and/or never.

CHARLOTTE. *I don't have time for another time and/or never.* I have a guy to murder, which will land me on the scaffold, which is why I came to you, which is why, as I yelled upon arrival, I NEED A LINE. My actions will be talked about for centuries and I don't want to sound like a dingbat. I need something that will sink into their memories for all time, something with a lot of "fuck you" in it. So. Playwright. Write.

OLYMPE. I mean…thank you for your enthusiasm but this isn't really my thing—

CHARLOTTE. COME ON. How many feminist playwrights do you think there are in Paris. *One. You.*

OLYMPE. And trust me that turning down an opportunity to tell someone what to say is *really* hard for me but I'm already juggling a lot now.

CHARLOTTE. Aren't we all: life, revolution, impossible beauty standards. *Help me.*

OLYMPE. I'm trying to help a lot of people…without leaving my office.

CHARLOTTE. Please. It's rare to be in the company of like minds in like corsets, and I know you're a "writery" kind of writer. So. If you write it? I'll say it, I'll shout it, I'll sing it.

OLYMPE. Sing it?

MARIANNE. NO.

CHARLOTTE. YES.

OLYMPE. Can you just gimme some context here. *What* exactly do you need written?

CHARLOTTE. Last words.

MARIANNE. Last words?

OLYMPE. Like…for a toast? Are you going to a wedding?

CHARLOTTE. No. I'm going to kill Jean-Paul Marat.
By stabbing.
Because he's awful.

MARIANNE. You're going to kill the journalist Marat?

CHARLOTTE. Yeah. Because he's awful.

OLYMPE. And by stabbing?!

CHARLOTTE. Yeah. Because he's awful.

OLYMPE. OK. Well. Now I *have* to write a play about her.

MARIANNE. *What about my pamphlets?*

OLYMPE. What about a torrid romance between a gorgeous assassin and a narcoleptic judge!

MARIANNE. *No.*

CHARLOTTE. What? No. I need *one* line, not a whole (and obviously terrible) play.

OLYMPE. *(Making a note.)* No I'm really seeing this. A woman willing to risk it all for vigilante justice. Yes!

MARIANNE. Should you maybe ask her *why* she's going to kill this guy before you make her a hero?

OLYMPE. I'm sure it's a good reason, look at that face. Now what if we call the play: "*The Young Assassin.*"

*Charlotte and Marianne make a "meh" sound.*

Or maybe just, "*Stabbing: The Musical*"! Oh this is gonna be great.

MARIANNE. Not anymore.

CHARLOTTE. Hold on, is she quoting me? Are you quoting me?

MARIANNE. Oh, theatre people don't quote, they embellish.

CHARLOTTE. Which would normally just be annoying, but this city is more than a little pissed off at the embellished or have you missed the last few beheadings. They don't like flourish.

OLYMPE. Theatre isn't flourish. It's fundamental.

MARIANNE. Here she goes.

OLYMPE. Story is the heartbeat of humanity and humanity gets really dark when the wrong stories are leading the people.

CHARLOTTE. Well I'm not here to make a *story*, I'm here to make *history*.

OLYMPE. History *is* a story. Just with…an extra…"hi."

MARIANNE. Stop.

OLYMPE. *(Using her hand as a puppet.)* Hi, Story!

MARIANNE. *We said no puppets.*

OLYMPE. Sorry.

CHARLOTTE. I don't think I was being clear. I'm an assassin. About to assassinate.

OLYMPE. And we'll get to that, but we have to do some character development first—

CHARLOTTE. I don't understand—

MARIANNE. It's all part of her creative process.

CHARLOTTE. I did not sign up for this.

OLYMPE. Because it's a *new* play—

CHARLOTTE. Oh god.

OLYMPE. Set during the French Revolution!

CHARLOTTE. I don't have time for—

OLYMPE. Starring lots of furious women!

CHARLOTTE. *(Being a furious woman.) I said I do not have time for such frivolity, I need some last words, and I need to sharpen my knife.*

*Charlotte reveals a long steak knife.*

*Pause.*

MARIANNE. Yeah. I'd watch a play about her.

OLYMPE. Right? What if she wears a sparkly mask?

CHARLOTTE. I'm not wearing a mask. I *want* people to know that I did it. Just. How long do I have to sit through this stupid play until we get to the murdering?

OLYMPE. Well, the exposition, rising action, it'll probably be a while.

MARIANNE. While we're waiting you could tell us your name?

CHARLOTTE. Right. Hi. Charlotte Corday.

OLYMPE. Spot on Charlotte Corday, a soon-to-be-killer in revolutionary France.

CHARLOTTE. Well don't say it like *that*. Not in that "You're a killer!" kind of way. Marat is a sick, fundamentalist, political *pundit* who has caused the deaths of thousands of innocent people with no tool as brave as a sword, no, he uses *words*. So really, I'm an editor.

OLYMPE. I wish I was that young and angry.

CHARLOTTE. Thank you, but you don't seem to get that I am on a deadline. That is not a pun but it could be. And I'm sure this performing art we're in the middle of is lovely but not lovelier than justifiable homicide, and I'm not sure if this *is* the play or if we're still in the prologue, because plays are only for rich people and chandeliers and I'm on a damn mission to maim, so if we're not actively avenging, can we get to the pointy point?

*Pause.*

OLYMPE. It's not for rich people.

CHARLOTTE. Theatre?

MARIANNE. I mean…

OLYMPE. No. It's just… I mean the chandeliers came with the space—

CHARLOTTE. So did the starving peasants outside.

OLYMPE. But I—no—the revolution just opened the theatres to the masses. Playwrights can finally write what they want. Theatre is democracy! Really pretty democracy with great hats and—Am I really writing for rich people?

MARIANNE. I mean…

CHARLOTTE. Yes. The ones who aren't fled or dead. Vigilante mobs always ruin the party. Isn't theatre just another party?

OLYMPE. No. It's culture.

CHARLOTTE. Isn't culture just another party?

OLYMPE. Culture is civilization! It's definitive, it lasts, the French are really into it! And I write pamphlets too, and we do a little community outreach and—oh god you're right.

MARIANNE. Ooh. She never says that.

OLYMPE. But art is all I know how to do. Truly. I'm useless in the sunshine. *(Getting annoyingly dramatic.)* Only *theatre* gives my soul—

CHARLOTTE. Ohmigod is this going to be a play about a play?

MARIANNE. *That* is the worst.

CHARLOTTE. That *is* the worst. Art about the rich is one thing, but art about rich people's art is too far.

MARIANNE. Agreed.

OLYMPE. Now wait just a minute, the performing arts are a vital part of—

CHARLOTTE. *Art and anything else that fakes its way through this life is useless to real human beings trying to fix the goddamn world.*

*Pause. Taken aback by her tone.*

OLYMPE. Well. It might be fiction, but it's not fake.
The beating hearts in front of you are real.
The gathering of people, the time spent is real.

MARIANNE. Agreed.

OLYMPE. The story is real when it starts.
And this story will capture our hearts.

CHARLOTTE. WHILE THE REIGN OF TERROR TAKES OUR HEADS.
Which I saw them do. To a hundred of my neighbors in one day.
Because Marat told them to.
This revolution is not for the people anymore, it's for the zealots.
They are taking over, and they are cruel, and you want to tell me a story? Do you see how insane that seems to a woman who is going to kill a man with her own hands? What the play is about does not matter. What is your life about? *That matters.*
Because sometimes? One man, every once in a while, *really needs to just die.*
Forget the line. I'll do it myself.

*Charlotte starts to go.*

MARIANNE. Are you in love with someone who doesn't love you back?

CHARLOTTE. NoWhyWouldYouSayThat? No. No.

MARIANNE. I sense the short temper of the unrequited.

OLYMPE. Oh *that's* what it is.

CHARLOTTE. I AM NOT THAT. You theatre people—you are so loose.

OLYMPE. *(Offended.)* I beg your— *(Not offended.)* That's accurate.

MARIANNE. So many egos, and tempers, and onstage heavily choreographed embraces.

OLYMPE. It's bound to spill over.

CHARLOTTE. Yeah. No. I'm gonna go.

OLYMPE. Don't go now we just started liking you.

CHARLOTTE. The nuns were right. Theatre is the devil's art.

OLYMPE. Because we get to decide who the real heroes are.

MARIANNE. The clergy just hate that.

CHARLOTTE. And. Who are the real heroes?

OLYMPE. We are. If I'm writing it.

MARIANNE. Stay. Your story's in good hands here.

*Pause. Charlotte likes the sound of that. She stays.*

CHARLOTTE. I could stay for a sec.

OLYMPE. Great. Now. My question is about plot.

MARIANNE. Me too. You're just gonna walk up to him and stab him? I mean just, stabstab?

OLYMPE. And because I'm seeing sequel potential, I'm worried about killing off our heroine so quickly.

MARIANNE. Agreed.

CHARLOTTE. No. I have to do this. I'm the only one with enough guts and cuteness to get away with this, so I will curl my hair, strap a steak knife to my thigh, use my sweet voice to infiltrate his house, stare him down and kill Jean-Paul Marat.
With said steak knife.
In his bathtub.

MARIANNE. His bathtub?

CHARLOTTE. He lives there. Skin condition.

OLYMPE. Ew.

CHARLOTTE. No, it'll be great. Intimate. Bloody. The water swirling red, the nudity. It'll be so…dramatic.

OLYMPE. Aha!

CHARLOTTE. *Not like that.*

OLYMPE. Drama wins!

CHARLOTTE. *I said dramatic not theatrical.*

OLYMPE. All the world's an audience.

CHARLOTTE. All the world's a mob.

MARIANNE. Sometimes it's hard to tell the difference.

CHARLOTTE. You know what? Never mind, I shouldn't have come.

OLYMPE. Charlotte, stop.

CHARLOTTE. No, no, the stories you trot out are distractions, and placating the rich, and full of *yelling and bosom and terrible dialogue*!

MARIANNE. *(Terribly serious.)* THEN WHY THE HELL ARE YOU HERE.

You know that a good deed needs a good story or else it might vanish like nothing. ever. happened.
You know that or else you wouldn't have shown up. You also know that her words are dangerous, she is putting her life on the line—

OLYMPE. I am?

MARIANNE. To tell a story that is good and good for the world—

OLYMPE. My *life* is on the line?

MARIANNE. She is risking everything for her art. So be nice to the playwright, because she holds fiction like you hold that blade and I know her weapon is sharper.

CHARLOTTE. Than a knife?

MARIANNE. Than any metal you've got. You tell me which one you want running the world.

*Pause. Olympe smiles at Marianne.*
*Charlotte looks at both of them…changes her mind.*

CHARLOTTE. I mean.
Sorry for the yelling.

MARIANNE. Uh-huh.

CHARLOTTE. And the aggressive entrance.

MARIANNE. Uh-huh.

CHARLOTTE. It's just. You two might be the first women I've ever like…liked. You're…interesting in like a…human kinda way.

MARIANNE. Thank you, young assassin.

OLYMPE. Such a good title.

CHARLOTTE. Do you mind if I hang here for half an hour until my appointment? You can maybe write my line while I practice my stabbing and scary eyes.

OLYMPE. Also a good title.

MARIANNE. Wait. You have an appointment to murder Marat?

CHARLOTTE. Well *he* doesn't know that's what it's for.
So don't let me get in your way. I don't know how this whole "drama" thing works. What do you—like—do all day?

OLYMPE. Well. I guess I…think up interesting people with enormous backstories and lots to lose and force them into action—

*Marie enters, looking lovely and startled.*

MARIE. Marie enters! Is she late? Or lost? What were they talking about? Was it her? It's always her. Or is she being her again? It's a confusing time. Hello. Marie… *(Whispered like it's a bad word.) Antoinette.*

CHARLOTTE. *Holy crap you're Marie-Antoinette?*

MARIE. *Isn't it exciting I'mSoFamous.*

MARIANNE. Infamous.

MARIE. *Famous.*

MARIANNE. Infamous.

CHARLOTTE. Wait. *You're the real Marie-Antoinette?*

MARIE. *I am so real!* Sigh. Sometimes I say it instead of doing it. It *used* to be so good to be real. Or did they always hate her? Did she mention her general confusion about this? She has no idea what's coming next, except that one day she woke up in a palace and went to sleep in a prison—not exactly prison—it was one of their lesser bedrooms—*with gunmen outside and no dessert!* The fear in her children's fancy eyes, trying to explain it to the dogs. The pressure, the amount of sudden exposition. It's all too much for Marie!

MARIANNE. And everyone watching her.

OLYMPE. Is there anything I can do for you, Majesty?

MARIE. I'm not even a "Majesty" anymore, the jerks.

MARIANNE. You're all Citizens now.

MARIE. But who wants a Citizen for a queen? That's ridiculous. *(To Olympe.)* I'm here for a rewrite.

OLYMPE. Oh god.

MARIE. Yes girl I need some help. First step: Make me Majesty again!

CHARLOTTE. Marat's the one who wanted to toss the monarchy. It all goes back to him.

OLYMPE. Exactly. There can be real reform *without* torching centuries of history.

MARIE. *Thank* you.

MARIANNE. But, come on, the royals aren't ready to change.

MARIE. No thank you.

MARIANNE. You aren't. You're dancing while Rome burns.

MARIE. First: It's Paris. Second: I had people dance *for* me. Third: We used to like me, the whole country would celebrate my birthday. How did it all turn into this rudeness and…murder.

MARIANNE. There's your title.

MARIE. Title? Whose title? I have so many titles.

OLYMPE. Not that kind of title.

CHARLOTTE. A play title. For a play.

MARIE. A *play* play? Which play? I'll play!

MARIANNE. It's her play. She's writing it.

OLYMPE. Yes. Olympe de Gouges, Your Majesty. Young playwright, activist, you might have heard of my moving political dramas—

MARIE. That's cute, no, I've heard that you're the only lady playwright left in Paris.

MARIANNE. And you need to rewrite your history because it makes you look bad.

MARIE. Most of it *does* make me look bad! You're hilarious.

MARIANNE. Not on purpose.

MARIE. Which is still hilarious! *(To Charlotte.)* You're pretty. And young. That must be fun. What are you?

CHARLOTTE. An assassin. It is fun.

MARIE. And who is your funny friend?

MARIANNE. Marianne Angelle. Not funny, not your friend, and we need to talk about colonization in the Caribbean right now.

MARIE. Caribbean? Ohmygod I *love* you guys.
Wait. Are you a…? Like a real live…? LikeASlave?

MARIANNE. *No.* I'm a free woman. My husband and I came to France to demand full and recognized civil and political equality. We want slavery abolished across the entire French Empire.

OLYMPE. *I am so for that.* CHARLOTTE. Yes We Can!

MARIE. You know it's the funniest thing, when I walked in here I could have sworn that you were my servant—

MARIANNE. I AM A FREE WOMAN OF MEANS LIKE YOU AND YOU AND YOU. I AM NO ONE'S SERVANT, I'M JUST STANDING NEARBY.

CHARLOTTE. I like her so much.

OLYMPE. She knows.

CHARLOTTE. *(To Marianne.)* I like you so much.

MARIANNE. I know.

*(To Marie.)* And you, Citizen, should know right now that the men and women of Saint-Domingue, who are dying in the sticky heat of your greed and oppression, the slaves who have suffered under your lash, have started a revolution of their own.

MARIE. Two revolutions? At once? Someone should have called ahead.

MARIANNE. It's the same revolution, the same rights, the same freedoms, just applied to your slaves instead of your peasants.

MARIE. I don't remember any of the other colonies acting this way.

MARIANNE. We know you need us. You people love our sugar, and coffee, and indigo—

MARIE. Indigo! For ribbons!

MARIANNE. So we have leverage. A country of our own and you get your coffee.

| CHARLOTTE. | OLYMPE. | MARIE. |
|---|---|---|
| Amazing. | Damn right. | Your coffee is really good. |

MARIE. I wish there was something I could do to help. But. I mean I couldn't even start a youth fitness program at the palace, and don't get me started on my rebranding ideas—*which were good.* I mean what *is* a fleur-de-lys? A sad flower? A terrible fork? No one listens to me unless I say something stupid, then it's the talk of the damn town.

MARIANNE. I feel your pain.

MARIE. Thank you.

CHARLOTTE. That was sarcasm.

MARIE. I realize that now.

OLYMPE. WAIT. Wait. I've got it. This is it. This is *it*!
THE QUEEN. CAN BE. IN THE PLAY.

| CHARLOTTE. | MARIANNE. | MARIE. |
|---|---|---|
| *My* play? *My play?!* | Oh *hell* no. What? Uh-uh. | I *would* likely make it more interesting. |

MARIANNE. Olympe, no. You were writing about revolution not royalty.

OLYMPE. Now wait, you said to write the intimate stories, that's what this would be. A woman at the edge of history, with everything to lose and nowhere to hide—

MARIE. Can it be a musical?

OLYMPE. Under all that vanity she's still just a person.

MARIE. Just a *fabulous* person.

OLYMPE. I mean it's not *her* fault that she's the queen.

MARIANNE. *Can we please not call her that anymore.* She's not my queen and she shouldn't be yours. She bankrupted your country!

MARIE. I mean we reduced a lot.

MARIANNE. The people have no food, and she had a palace!

MARIE. So did the dogs—mini ones—hilarious.

MARIANNE. She is everything wrong with a class of people so vacant-hearted that they can't see the horror of their own luxury.

MARIE. OK I had no choice in becoming royalty, it was thrown at me. And by that I mean a mountain of free stuff and undeserved compliments. What would you do? *You'd take them. They're free.* But just to be very clear, I did *not* say that bit about the cake. That was out of context. I thought I was ordering lunch.

CHARLOTTE. Cake for lunch?

MARIE. Uh, *all* lunch comes with cake.

MARIANNE. *And all cake comes with sugar and all sugar comes from families dying in the drowning heat a world away.* Figurehead or actual head it's *hers* that should roll, not ours.

*Marie is silent. Marianne didn't mean to go that far.*

MARIE. *(Sincere.)* I know what most people think of me. It's not very nice. And I deserve...some of it. And I have a feeling I might die sooner than later, but I would very much like Later to know that I was a real person. Who bled and gave birth in a closed room with two hundred people watching so give me a little credit here. I just... I care. I care so much about my people and my country. I just need better press. You can do that for me Madame De Gouges. I was hoping that you would. I would be honored to be in your play. *(To Marianne.)* And try to earn your respect. Via meaningful connection...and minor revisionism.

OLYMPE. I know I shouldn't but I kind of like her.

MARIANNE. She's not worthy, Olympe. She doesn't belong with us. She is not a revolutionist.

CHARLOTTE. Yeah, what would your declaration be? "We hold these *jewels* to be self-evident."

MARIE. Well they are.

CHARLOTTE. So shiny.

MARIE. Did you say declaration? Like the Americans? They do *great* declarations. I know Thomas Jefferson if you want any advice. He'd like you. *(To Marianne.)* Actually he'd like *you*.

MARIANNE. *I feel like that should make me really mad. You need to go.*

OLYMPE. Wait—What if she could help us?

MARIANNE. Help us? Help *us*? No.

MARIE. I mean sometimes a revolution needs a woman's touch.

CHARLOTTE. Or you know...stabstab.

MARIANNE. It does need a woman's touch, but that is not a soft thing, Citizen Cake.

MARIE. *(Showing her dominatrix side.)* Oh. I know it's not. Not at night, not in secret, not when you're a tall, red-haired American diplomat in my goddamn country. Then it is a hard hand that knows your every weakness, and is firm and red and shuts you up and makes you sit and you better do what it says or else you're damn right there'll be a revolution.

*Pause. The others are surprised and impressed.*

| MARIANNE. | CHARLOTTE. | OLYMPE. |
|---|---|---|
| I mean... | She is kinda awesome. | Yeah I really like her. |

MARIE. Question. Are there snacks? I'm used to a lot of snacking. Treats? Sweets? Anything? Nothing?

CHARLOTTE. I have a mint.

*Charlotte takes out a plastic-wrapped mint.*
*Hands it to Marie.*

MARIE. A mint! How darling. *Merci, mademoiselle!* Now tell us of our play, Madame De Gouges.

OLYMPE. Oh. Well I haven't started writing anything just yet but—

MARIE. Let the synopsis begin!

OLYMPE. OK. Um. Well. Think of the power of a play that shows the entwined lives of real women—

*Marie starts to open the mint—the wrapper crackles.*
*Olympe stops, Marie stops.*

Women who, even through their differences—

*Marie's mint wrapper crackles. Olympe stops. Marie stops.*

join forces to protest the deep injustice of—

*Marie crackles the hell out of that wrapper—*

| MARIANNE. | CHARLOTTE. | OLYMPE. |
|---|---|---|
| That is so loud. | OHMYGOD, STOP. | Can you figure that out, Your Majesty? |

MARIE. *Sometimes good things make a lot of noise.*

OLYMPE. See? Musical.

| MARIANNE. | CHARLOTTE. | MARIE. |
|---|---|---|
| No. | No. | Yay! |

*Marie frees the mint, pops it in her mouth, smiles.*

OLYMPE. OK look. I don't know what I'm writing just yet, but I know that our voices deserve the stage. We deserve to be our own heroes, everyone's heroes. We're all of us more alike than we are different, and if this revolution is what I think it is? This is our time to be known, and heard, and—

CHARLOTTE. *(Checking her watch.)* Oh crap I have to go kill a guy.

OLYMPE. Come on, that speech was getting good.

MARIE. You're killing a guy? Which one?

MARIANNE. Marat in the bathtub with a steak knife.

MARIE. Oh kill him! I hate that man! He put my name on a list. *With other people.* Can you imagine? You know my husband, he always said Marat was a bloodlusty wacko. And then he chops my husband's head off. That shows how right he was.

OLYMPE. OK but—Charlotte. What if you miss? What if he gets you first?

CHARLOTTE. Steak knife pretty much always beats naked-guy-in-a-bath.

OLYMPE. And he deserves it, but you don't. We don't want to lose you. Don't do this.

CHARLOTTE. Then who will. The entire city is scared of him. Well I'm not.

MARIANNE. That's right, girl. I got your back.

OLYMPE. *Marianne.*

MARIE. Me too, me too! StabStabStab!

OLYMPE. Would you stop encouraging her. I'm trying to save her life, because there is no doubt that *she will die for this.*

CHARLOTTE. AND THAT DOES NOT SCARE ME.
Not for this.
I am not afraid to die for this.

*Pause.*

OLYMPE. What's that like?

*Pause.*

CHARLOTTE. Like knowing your lines.

*Pause.*

MARIE. Does she love someone who doesn't love her back?

| CHARLOTTE. | OLYMPE. | MARIANNE. |
| --- | --- | --- |
| WHY DOES THAT MATTER? God, that has *nothing to do with—* | Yes she does. | That's what I said. |

MARIE. Is it your tutor? Is his name Jacques? I know these things.

OLYMPE. Just wait, Charlotte.

CHARLOTTE. No. Jacques knows what he did.

OLYMPE. I'm talking about Marat. The little assassination you're about to attempt. Have you really thought this through? Have you thought about Madame Guillotine?

CHARLOTTE. Well yeah, who hasn't.

MARIE. I hate that bitch.

MARIANNE. It's the efficiency that most offends me.

MARIE. Too quick.

OLYMPE. Too easy.

MARIANNE. They say it's egalitarian.

MARIE. Bullshit, it's cheap.

OLYMPE. I mean take some care.

MARIANNE. We're not cattle.

CHARLOTTE. To them we are.

OLYMPE. Carting you through the city to your doom.

MARIANNE. In a wagon.

MARIE. No grandeur.

OLYMPE. Trash at you.

MARIANNE. They cut your hair.

CHARLOTTE. They cut my hair?

OLYMPE. Weren't you aware?

CHARLOTTE. No! That's not fair!

MARIANNE. Maybe it could be a musical.

OLYMPE. *(To Charlotte.)* Just think about this. If you die? They could vilify you, call you witch or make him a martyr. Then it's like Marat wins.

CHARLOTTE. Which is why you have to tell my story so they understand it.
And do *not* let them cut my hair.

OLYMPE. But. We didn't get you your last line. It might take a while. A long while.

CHARLOTTE. Then I'm gonna have to go with: "May God have no pity, you motherfuckers."

| OLYMPE. | MARIE. | MARIANNE. |
|---|---|---|
| Lemme work on that. | Hilarious! | I mean… |

MARIANNE. You could always sing. That's what I'd do. A song sticks.

CHARLOTTE. A song? That's not a bad idea.

OLYMPE. You said no musicals!

MARIE. What about the writer's last words? That must be a lot of pressure since that's kind of your thing.

OLYMEPE. I don't need last words, I am of the theatre, we just go on and on. And on.

MARIE. But you must've thought about what you'd say if they—

OLYMPE. I DON'T KNOW.
I don't know.

*Pause.*

MARIE. Well. I do hope that my last words are sympathetic. I just don't want to sound silly because I AM STILL THE GODDAMN QUEEN OF FRANCE NO MATTER WHAT THOSE FUCKERS SAY.
And I. Will die. Royally.
Do you have another mint?

CHARLOTTE. No.

MARIE. *Shit.*

OLYMPE. Charlotte we can find another way to stop Marat—a protest, a scathing farce—

CHARLOTTE. Thank you, but…it's what you said. We're all in a play that someone else is writing.

OLYMPE. Did I say that?

CHARLOTTE. And I am certain that this is my cue.

MARIANNE. A word of advice, young assassin, aim high and strike deep.

OLYMPE. Wait. Charlotte—

MARIE. And tie back your hair. I know a little about stabbing.

*Marie gives Charlotte a red ribbon like it's a secret weapon.*

OLYMPE. *Charlotte.*

CHARLOTTE. Thank you, ladies. Gotta go make some…
Hi, story.

*Olympe smiles—that was her line!—as Charlotte exits.*

*Marianne grabs paper and pen and she follows Charlotte.*

MARIANNE. OK. I think this might be worth writing home about.
*(To Olympe.)* You, keep writing.
*(To Marie.)* You, keep quiet.

*Marianne exits after Charlotte.*

MARIE. Enjoy your exit.

*Marie picks up the book Charlotte left.*

Oh, the little murderer left her book. Plutarch. *Parallel Lives.* Hilarious.

*Olympe thinks and thinks...*
*Marie is expectant but still.*

So...
I generally just wait until someone comes to get me...
Or I hear trumpets. I usually have to go if I hear trumpets.

*She listens. No trumpets.*

I'm good.

OLYMPE. *(Distracted but polite.)* Uh-huh.

MARIE. Or maybe I'm not good at all. Is it hot in here or is that just...mortality. Or sudden lack of sugar. And coffee. And husband. Not a great king. But a man. He's at least a man, you know? You shouldn't need to be great to be spared.

OLYMPE. *(Distracted but polite.)* Uh-huh.

MARIE. When did it all turn so cruel? Did I do this? Be honest, you seem honest. Is all of this because of me?

OLYMPE. Not...exactly.

MARIE. But did I make it worse? I did, didn't I. Am I...too pretty?

*Olympe is on thin ice...*

OLYMPE. Definitely too pretty.

MARIE. I thought so. Maybe if I change my hair, or perhaps less bosom?

OLYMPE. That would be a public service.

MARIE. Ugh. God. It's always the women who have to do the changing, isn't it?

OLYMPE. What did you say?

MARIE. Oh you know. Change this, Change that, ChangeYourEntirePersonalityAndAllegiance.
What about what *we* want? You know? I could tell you a few things I'd like to change and they are *not* my last name.
Now for the play, would you write me with different hair? I'd like to do my part for the cause.

OLYMPE. I don't think…I'm going to write a play anymore.

MARIE. Oh. I thought this was scene one?

OLYMPE. It was. And then it wasn't, then it was, now it's not again.

MARIE. That makes sense.

OLYMPE. *(An idea is forming, a good one.)* It does actually. Because we don't write what we know, we write what we want. And you're right, we don't need to change, *they* need to change.

MARIE. I'm right?! Gasp! Sometimes I say it instead of doing it.

OLYMPE. Yes. I can't waste time on a play—Marianne's right—A Declaration! For the Rights of Women! I could just take Thomas Paine's declaration and switch the gender. Oh that's great. See? OK—

MARIE. I starting to think this might not be OK.

OLYMPE. I will not only *write* this Declaration, I will *declare* this Declaration!

MARIE. Wait—

OLYMPE. Theatre and politics coming together!

MARIE. You thought they were separate?

OLYMPE. I will go to the National Assembly myself, and stand up and—

MARIE. You're going to the Assembly? In person? On purpose? Girl. Hold up. They're awful, they're overrun by Jacobins, like frothy mean Extremists that killed my husband. They will not like this.

OLYMPE. What good is a declaration if everyone already agrees?

MARIE. Yeah I'm really not seeing this ending well.

OLYMPE. It never ends well unless you write the ending yourself. If I have the right to die by their hand, I have the right to speak my mind. And I will.

*Olympe starts to write…and write…*

MARIE. I mean… Sigh.

*Transition…*

## TWO.

*Charlotte…*
*Standing beside a bright white claw-foot tub*
*full of water.*
*She holds the knife. She wears her red ribbon.*
*She recites her letter.*

CHARLOTTE. It is to you, the good people of France, that I must define these actions. I am doing this with the full knowledge that I will be soon in the quiet arms of Madame Guillotine, but…Jean-Paul Marat, by eight o'clock tonight, shall be dead.

*Switch to Olympe…*

*Olympe stands at a podium in a loud, cavernous room*
*full of angry men.*
*She reads with verve:*

OLYMPE. When will women ask ourselves… What has this Revolution given *us*? And if the answer is *nothing*? When will we take it for ourselves?

CHARLOTTE. Until Marat is silenced, you, my friends, will live in danger. So. I will avenge us all.

OLYMPE. So. I now present this Declaration of the Rights of Woman and the Female Citizen.
Article One: Woman is born free and lives equal to man.

*Male objection resounds! Olympe stands there, breathing in the moment.*

CHARLOTTE. As the murderer Marat draws his final breath, there will at last be peace in France.
You're welcome.
Charlotte Corday.

*With a swift strike Charlotte "kills" Marat*

*and the water in the tub bloodies.*
*She stands there, bloody, breathing in the moment.*

*Switch to Marianne…*

*Marianne reads a letter.*

MARIANNE. My dear Vincent,
We fight for this better world *together* even if we are a world away.
I fight harder with you in my heart.
More news of the Paris revolution enclosed. Be safe and write soon.

*She stands there breathing in the paper and the memory of her husband.*

*Blackout on Olympe.*
*Blackout on Charlotte.*
*Blackout on Marianne.*

*Switch to Marie…*

*To no one…except maybe her ribbons.*

MARIE. So here's what I don't get. Isn't the definition of *a revolution* "the turning about of an object on a central axis thereby landing its journeyman in the same exact spot whereon they started"? Because that seems like a waste of *everyone's* time.

*Which transitions to…*

## THREE.

*Marie still waiting, playing with some ribbon.*

*Marianne runs in…*
*They had both hoped to not be alone with each other.*
*They make each other nervous…*

MARIANNE. It's happening. It's all happening. *Olympe?*

MARIE. Nope. Lady writer left a while ago.

MARIANNE. So. It's just…me and Marie-Antoinette.

MARIE. Is it ever *just* Marie-Antoinette. Ribbon?

MARIANNE. Why don't you keep it.

MARIE. Oh, I was going to.

MARIANNE. Excuse me, I have to go do something useful.—

MARIE. *PleaseDon'tLeaveMeI'mScared.*

*Marianne stops.*

It's so...lively out there.
Unless you're Marat.

MARIANNE. Touché, Citizen.

MARIE. I made a touché?! I've always wanted to do that.
Wait. That means she did it? She killed him? Did you see it? Was it awesome? She is such a badass. Or a crazy person. I mean, the chutzpah of that girl. And such good hair. Tell me everything.

MARIANNE. I mean... OK, she walks right in, front door, I'm watching from the street, it's quiet for a few minutes, and then I hear her yell "FOR FRANCE!," then this scream and splash, and the white curtains spackle red. Commotion in the house, the housekeeper wails, the authorities rush in, then they take a perfectly collected Charlotte Corday to prison in a cart. She was amazing. Perfect form, flawless execution.

MARIE. Touché too!

MARIANNE. Touché too.

*They smile. They don't mean to become friends but perhaps they are.*
*Marie is oddly profound...*

MARIE. I fear we shall not know the rightness of our revolutions nor the heroes of our stories for generations to come.

*Marianne registers this profundity with surprised respect. Pause.*

MARIANNE. Uh. Yeah. Exactly. That was—

MARIE. Unexpectedly profound. It happens sometimes.

*Marie might play with her ribbons like a kitten...*

And...you're, like, *not* a queen?

MARIANNE. No. Revolutionary. And a mom.

MARIE. A mom, me too! I forget about that sometimes, but I am. How old are your kids?

MARIANNE. Well Annabelle is ten.

MARIE. Awww. Lots of bows?

MARIANNE. She loves bows. On everything—the cat, the teacups.

MARIE. Me too! Teacup bows are the best!

MARIANNE. And Vincent is eight. He's named after his dad.

MARIE. So are mine. Isn't it funny when they start talking alike—father and son? I just think it's so funny. They sneeze the same. They say "spoon" the same. Hilarious. And now sad.

MARIANNE. The world found it just despicable. No nation, no matter how revolutionary, should kill a king that way.

MARIE. Aw, thanks. I mean. He was a lumpy man, but he had good moments. I didn't dislike him. In fact I liked him, when he would just stand there looking serious. He was best when he was just…standing.

MARIANNE. How did you meet?

MARIE. On our wedding day. I wasn't supposed to marry him, you know. But all the rest of my sisters had smallpox so it fell to me. Which was fine. I mean the finery was exquisite. Everything else was a bit strained. You know we didn't consummate the damn thing for *three goddamned years*? Can you imagine? *The tension?* And the whole country blames me! And I'm like "nuh uh! I'm totally down! He's the one who—" Turns out? He had to have an operation on his Little Prince before he could—Yeah. So that was anti-hilarious. Then finally little Marie-Thérèse came along, then little Louis-Joseph, then little Louis-Charles, then little Sophie poor dear. Then they killed him. In the square that used to be named after his grandfather. The rest is… I talk too much. What about your husband?

MARIANNE. Oh. We don't have to…

MARIE. No please tell me. It's so nice to pretend nothing is wrong in the world. Is yours a love story? I love love stories.

MARIANNE. It is a love story.

MARIE. Brava, then. *Allons-y.*

MARIANNE. Well. Vincent is a catch. He's strong, and tall, with these eyes that just make you tell him every little thing.

MARIE. Ooh.

MARIANNE. And he doesn't walk. Oh no. Vincent *strides.* Long legs and swinging arms, you know.

MARIE. *(Getting a little too excited.)* Uh-huh.

MARIANNE. And when that man wears a suit? Just give up, just don't even try to look away. But when he takes it *off*?

MARIE. TELL ME EVERYTHING.

MARIANNE. He courted me for months, but the truth is I thought he was too handsome.

MARIE. Too handsome is not a thing.

MARIANNE. Well, you don't want them *that* dashing, it'd make me worry.

MARIE. Not me—Dash Dash! OK, Vincent is a dream, he swings his arms, when is le smooch?

MARIANNE. Well I kept thinking "yes, he's very nice" and "yes he's from a good family." But I just wasn't sure I *really knew* him. Until. He let loose this *laugh.* We were talking about—I don't know—and out comes this rumbly, and loud, and big-old-stupid laugh.

*Might we hear this laugh?*

And that's when I agreed to marry him.

MARIE. That is literally hilarious!

MARIANNE. They're perfect when they're just a little flawed. You know?

MARIE. I do *not* know, but that sounds so fun!

MARIANNE. I miss him. And our kids, they're with my mom. Revolutions aren't for children.

MARIE. Work-life balance, I get it.

MARIANNE. It's hard. When Vincent went back to Saint-Domingue last month I…I knew it was the right thing. But even when we're apart for a day. I miss him.

MARIE. What's that like?

MARIANNE. Like. Sending a letter to your best friend that keeps getting returned.

*Marianne's expression darkens. Something's wrong. Marie awkwardly pats Marianne's hand.*

MARIE. I don't usually comfort other people, am I doing it right?

MARIANNE. You're doing fine.

MARIE. Love letters lost…that is the saddest thing in the world. You know you could use one of my ships to find him? I think I still have some ships. I used to wear them in my hair, little ones with sails and everything, which does seem a bit excessive in retrospect. Anyway, we'll find out what happened—

MARIANNE. I think… I think he might be dead.

MARIE. *What?*

MARIANNE. I think they might have killed him.

MARIE. Oh my god.

MARIANNE. I don't know if they did but I swear I can tell that something is wrong, is profoundly and terribly…gone. And I don't know what to do. What do I do? Do I leave? Do I stay? What do I do?

*Marie hugs her like a best friend. A perfect comfort.*

MARIE. I understand this feeling. Don't go.

*Marianne is surprised by the relief she feels telling someone.*

MARIANNE. We each carry a final letter to the other in case something happens to one of us. So we know.

*Marianne takes out a red-ribboned letter—hers to Vincent.*

MARIE. This is his?

MARIANNE. No. Mine to him. I haven't seen his yet—

MARIE. Well there you go. Hope. Because we will not give up on him, we will find him.
And I will help you with everything I have left, Citizen Marianne.

*She hands her some ribbons. Marianne actually means this…*

MARIANNE. Thank you, Citizen Majesty.

*Marie is stunned and appreciative.*

*Olympe enters with—*

OLYMPE. GoddammitGoddammit*Goddammit*. I'm gonna let you ladies guess how my little solo show at the National Assembly went?

MARIE. Um… Poorly!

OLYMPE. Poorly does not properly convey the reviews it received. They booed me. *Hundreds of men booed me as I spoke.*

MARIE. Well, what good is a declaration if everyone already agrees.

OLYMPE. Well they could agree *a little*. How can these men hate a declaration of women's *equality* when that's exactly what *Egalité* is!

MARIANNE. But *Fraternité* it is not.

OLYMPE. *Goddammit.* What the hell is this revolution about? Ugh. World changing should be easier.

MARIE. I mean, my wig choices have done it on numerable occasions, *(Talking about Vincent.)* but we were just talking and Marianne is worried about—

MARIANNE. *(Deliberately not talking about Vincent.)* Marie don't, just—

MARIE. What?

MARIANNE. There's no need to say anything—

OLYMPE. What's going on?

MARIE. Her husband.

OLYMPE. What about him?

MARIE. She's worried that something might have happened to him.

OLYMPE. Marianne, what's she talking about?

MARIANNE. I…I haven't heard from him in weeks. Something's not right. I don't know anything for sure but—

OLYMPE. Have you seen his last letter? The last letter he keeps for you?

MARIANNE. No, but—

OLYMPE. Then I'm sure he's fine. You'd know if he wasn't.

MARIANNE. Yes, but it's just strange that he hasn't—

OLYMPE. Don't worry before there's a problem. There's enough going on already. You should have seen the way those men at the Assembly glared at me. One guy threw a shoe. I mean it's so obvious what I was asking for and they wouldn't even hear me out. Maybe I start killing people like Charlotte. That seems to make them listen.

MARIE. It's making people *talk*, not listen.

OLYMPE. I just can't believe she actually did it.

MARIE. I can. That girl. She has some—

OLYMPE. Conviction.

MARIE. Cheekbones.

MARIANNE. Upper body leverage.

OLYMPE. I wish I had her certainty.

MARIE. You mean cheekbones.

OLYMPE. *(To Marianne.)* Ladies, I can't help but think this revolution might not be for us anymore. But I want it to be, I want to have faith in justice.

MARIANNE. I do.

OLYMPE. In common sense.

MARIE. I do not.

OLYMPE. *In a good story.* But what are they doing for us at the moment? Not much. Makes me want to abandon everything

MARIANNE. No. Don't say that. You need to remind yourself what we're fighting for: conviction, sacrifice for the greater good. Come with me to see Charlotte.

MARIE. To a prison? Oh no. I'm afraid they'll never let me out.

MARIANNE. Olympe, come on. She needs us.

OLYMPE. She needs us to be implicated and die with her? I don't think so.

MARIANNE. She needs you to tell her story.

OLYMPE. I will. From here.

MARIANNE. You're really that scared.

OLYMPE. I'm not scared.

MARIE. You sound a little scared.

MARIANNE. And you cannot give up now, none of us can. Because it seems like it's going to get worse—

MARIE. A lot worse.

MARIANNE. Before it gets better.

MARIE. Not that much better.

MARIANNE. And that's when this country is going to need us the most. Especially the writers. When they give up all is truly lost.

OLYMPE. I mean I'd like to tell her story, I liked her, but it stopped being fun when she actually killed someone. Now it's totally different than I was going to write it. Reality messed up my narrative.

MARIE. I hate when that happens.

MARIANNE. You don't always get to pick the ending but it doesn't mean it's not a good story. She needs her friends now.

OLYMPE. Well we really just met her.

MARIANNE. She needs a dramaturg.

OLYMPE. Don't we all.

MARIANNE. She needs the last words you promised her.

*Pause. Olympe writes on a slip of paper and gives it to Marianne.*

OLYMPE. OK. Give her this. If I'd had more time it would've rhymed.

MARIE. Is she good on ribbons? 'Cause I have a few extra if, y'know, that might beat back the tide of fate coming hard against us all.

MARIANNE. *(To Olympe.)* I'm just saying…for a dramatist you seem awfully scared of drama.

*Marianne exits.*

MARIE. Ooh. Would you write me an exit line like that? I've always wanted to be like—"blah blah blah RETORT" and then just leave and the scene is—like—*over.*

*Pause. Olympe glares.*

*Blackout.*

## FOUR.

*Charlotte in a prison cell.*
*Marianne is visiting her.*

CHARLOTTE. And after all the shoving and the yelling, they get me to the prison. And I'm exhausted right? And then they had to check my *virginity*, of course. And they were like "She's a virgin!" And I was like "not after you checked, I'm not." And it wasn't the intimate violation of it that bugged me—though I swear to god some guy hit on me *on the way to prison*—It was that they were *sure* there was a man involved. "She wouldn't have avenged her people on her own, she must have been fucked into it." I mean Jesus Christ a girl can't even assassinate someone without judgment. I'm joining Olympe's group.

MARIANNE. What's Olympe's group?

CHARLOTTE. I heard that she declared something at the Assembly. Some big women's group? For girls to go scouting or something?

MARIANNE. I don't think that's what she was—

CHARLOTTE. Oh yeah, that's what they were saying in my virginity check.

MARIANNE. No, it was a Declaration for all Women. *Egalité* means equality for everyone, that's her point.

CHARLOTTE. Exactly what I'm saying! Who checks the boys' virginity when they go to prison for murder, huh? *No one.* That'd be equality, that'd be…something…good.

MARIANNE. You OK?

CHARLOTTE. Me? Fine. Good. I mean… I did the deed. Stabbity-Stab, he's dead, what I wanted. So…yeah.

MARIANNE. You know, they're calling you the Angel of Assassins.

CHARLOTTE. Oooh. Really? That's not bad.

MARIANNE. Yeah, kind of a girl-next-door-meets-Joan-of-Arc vibe.

CHARLOTTE. Nice. Wait. They think I'm crazy?

MARIANNE. No.

CHARLOTTE. Because Joan of Arc was kinda crazy. I'm not crazy, I'm fed up, I *had* to kill him, it was a civic duty…that felt fucking awesome. I mean the *feel* of it? Of righteous vengeance is just… floral, like a blooming of power and rightness and—goddammit it's what sex must feel like.

MARIANNE. I mean…

CHARLOTTE. The way that man looked at me with my knife in his chest. I was this close to him, his breath on my lips, leaning into him, and I said—I actually said this—"You. Die. Now."
But that's not crazy that's…just very literal.

MARIANNE. I mean…

CHARLOTTE. Did I tell you some guy's painting my portrait? That's kinda cool. Wait till Jacques sees that. Fucker. And people are reading my letter? The last line might have been a bit much but I didn't have Olympe's help.

MARIANNE. Yes it's circulating in a pamphlet. Widely. But…

CHARLOTTE. What.

MARIANNE. There's also some…celebration…of Marat.

CHARLOTTE. *Wait what?*

MARIANNE. Now this was bound to happen, but some idiots are trying to turn him into a martyr.

CHARLOTTE. Some? I mean…not *many*, not *some*. A faction. A small but vocal faction? Right?

MARIANNE. …right.

*Hard pause.*

CHARLOTTE. Well. Sometimes history judges slowly.
My trial is tomorrow. It'd be nice to see a familiar face. I am preparing my Steely Look of Unwavering Calm, but I may need a high-five before I go onstage.

MARIANNE. You mean on trial.

CHARLOTTE. Same thing. All the world's an audience.

MARIANNE. Are you quoting Olympe at me?

CHARLOTTE. Am I? Oh god. Never tell her this.

MARIANNE. I would never.

*They share a smile.*

And I'll be at the trial. You're an example for us all to keep fighting, do what we have to, even if it means being very…literal.

*Charlotte lets the upset overwhelm her—tears even.*

CHARLOTTE. Would you. Please fight for me too. I don't think I finished the job.

MARIANNE. I don't know if we'll ever finish it.

CHARLOTTE. But I don't even know if I helped. *Like at all.* What if I just made it worse? Oh god, am I crazy? Did I do the right thing? I mean I know technically murder is wrong most of the time but—oh god this is not—oh god—

MARIANNE. As a wise and weird woman once said: We may not know the rightness of our revolutions nor the heroes of our stories for generations to come.
But I think you're one of them. And I will carry you into every fray I can find.

*The sound of approaching men unlocking steel doors.*
*They're coming for her.*

CHARLOTTE. OK tell people—tell them—I don't know. I'm not great with words. Tell Olympe to find the words.

MARIANNE. She found these.

*Marianne hands her a slip of paper.*

CHARLOTTE. For me? Really? Oh thank you, *thank you.*

MARIANNE. Don't thank me. Or her. It was literally the least she could do.

CHARLOTTE. No it's not. It's everything. Absolutely everything.

MARIANNE. *(Re: her new line.)* Now when you say that… Look up, find your light, and say it loud.

CHARLOTTE. OK. Um. I'm really scared.

MARIANNE. Of course you are. And that's OK.

CHARLOTTE. I'm so scared.

MARIANNE. I know. But don't let anyone else know it. You're brave, and ready, and not alone. Good work, young assassin.

CHARLOTTE. Thank you. Thank you.

*Beat. The ending builds out of Charlotte's preparing for death.*

OK.
OK.

*Across town Olympe holds her pen, trying to tame her ideas.*
*Across town Marianne holds her final letter to Vincent.*
*And Marie listens for trumpets and caresses her ribbons.*

| MARIANNE. | CHARLOTTE. | OLYMPE. | MARIE. |
|---|---|---|---|
| OK. | OK. | OK. | OK. |

*Blackout.*

**End of Act One**

## ACT TWO

### ONE.

*Olympe starts this scene in a rush,*
*writing in her study with furious inspiration…*

OLYMPE. OK, yeah, this is going to start moving really fast now. Marat's death has made things very bad, very quickly. The revolution has turned violent, anything done or said against the Republic is now treason and treason is punished by death. There are mobs in the streets, Marat's a martyr, Charlotte's on trial, and I've finally found something to write about—!

*Marie reads over her shoulder.*

MARIE. Marie! OhMyGod, is that *me* Marie? The *Queen* Marie? The Me Queen?!

OLYMPE. Yes, can you not yell *all* of your revelations as you have them.

MARIE. Gasp! Sigh! Retort! Oh that seems like *such* the right move.

OLYMPE. Well the declaration was a bust and you're really interesting.

MARIE. Right?

OLYMPE. Back to plays. Fiction I can fix. Reality is way too hard to write. At least drama has some structure. We're headed somewhere clear. And I have to admit that this play might be good. Like actually good.

MARIE. And it's really about me? That's hilarious!

OLYMPE. Actually, it's a very serious epic historical political drama with a few songs that will be a vindication for generations! Because it will last five hours.

MARIE. *Ugh.* But the title. Something cute, something that says "She's Innocent!" Perhaps, "*The Lovely Queen*" or maybe, "*Braveheart.*"

OLYMPE. NO. It has to be sweeping and profound. Something like… "*France Preserved*"!

MARIE. Sounds delicious.

OLYMPE. *(A better title.)* OK maybe… "France *Saved*."

MARIE. Oh that's nice. I'm thinking "Ooh, is France an ingénue tied to a train track? And what are trains?"

OLYMPE. *(The extended title.)* "*France Saved; or, A Tyrant Dethroned*." There we go, that's it.

MARIE. De-WhatNow? De*throned*? Who's dethroned?

OLYMPE. I want a country that owns itself and I don't think we can do that with a monarchy so this play—

MARIE. *Silence.* No queen? That is not—no—wait. Do I die in the end?

OLYMPE. Well I haven't written the end.

MARIE. You said "we're headed somewhere clear, drama has structure." Well where the hell are we headed and why is it not a beach?

OLYMPE. Look—

MARIE. No *you* look. I'm the main character of this thing, right? So let's make me stay queen and not die, OK? *Let's do that.*

OLYMPE. Sometimes the story tells itself.

MARIE. THEN YOU BETTER TELL THIS DAMN STORY TO BEHAVE.
I have precious little time to force history to like me. *Now tell me what you're writing.*

OLYMPE. I don't have time to go back, I'm halfway through the story.

MARIE. *Aren't we all. Tell me.*

*Pause.*

OLYMPE. Setting: The queen's private chamber in the palace on the eve of the fall of the monarchy.

MARIE. That's a bad day to set a romantic comedy.

OLYMPE. It's not a romantic comedy.

*Marie whines, Olympe pushes through it.*

You're desperate. You're plotting any way to uphold the crumbling royal institution while the revolutionary forces are at your door.

MARIE. *(Like she's talking to a scary movie.)* Get away from the door Marie!

OLYMPE. Then a woman comes to you, to convince you to let go of the old ways and embrace the new, to compromise. Her name is Olympe.

MARIE. Hold the throne. You're writing about yourself now?

OLYMPE. It's a character.

MARIE. Named after you.

OLYMPE. Well yes but—

MARIE. Isn't that confusing? I'm confused. I hate when theatre confuses me.

OLYMPE. I call it "Meta Theatre." The point is to be a little confusing.

MARIE. I hate it. I already hate it.

OLYMPE. You don't hate it.

MARIE. The play is trash!

OLYMPE. *The play could save us both.*

*Pause.*

MARIE. *Comment? (French: "How?")*

OLYMPE. By showing *you* learning a goddamn lesson for starters. By showing people that revolutions needn't be so bloody.
That they can be kind and creative. I'm telling you, Your Majesty,
This play. Will be. Important.

MARIE. If it's not a romantic comedy nobody will come.

OLYMPE. I'll add a butler.

MARIE. Hilarious!

OLYMPE. Now, the first act ends with Olympe convincing the queen to work *with* the revolutionaries to create a Constitutional Monarchy that truly embraces Liberté, Egalité—

MARIE. Sororité.

OLYMPE. *Yes.* The country is saved by its women.

*Beat.*

MARIE. That I like. Keep writing. And if you want…the production may borrow my wigs.

OLYMPE. I'll make sure to thank you in the program.

*Marie suddenly hugs Olympe like a child hugging a mother.*

*Olympe is shocked, then hugs her back.*

MARIE. It's finality that scares me most.

OLYMPE. That's the hardest part. Writing the ending.

MARIE. *Oui. C'est vrai.* That was my fear as a child. Never seeing people again. Or dogs. How are you supposed to understand when you're so young? Never? What is "never"?
Never is now, Young Marie. Never might be now.

OLYMPE. I don't know, Your Majesty. Never might not come to you. You're a very compelling woman. I'm the one that should worry. My attempt at immortality is on paper, scripts in actors' pockets. It's not as glamorous as it looks.

MARIE. Oh, don't worry, it doesn't look very glamorous.
But I like your stories. I'll remember them. And I'll tell my grandchildren and they'll tell their grandchildren, and their grandchildren will invent new ways to watch never-ending plays on ever-tinier stages. May I nap on you?

*Marie fills her lap with the growing pile of ribbons that are now a pillow for Marie.*

OLYMPE. A play that doesn't end. If I'm writing what I really want? That'd be it.

MARIE. Then tell me that story, and let's not have an ending, shall we? A cliffhanger will do. Something that makes you want to come back for more and more and…

*Olympe inhales to begin her a story but—*
*Marianne runs in.*

MARIANNE. They lied—there was no trial—Charlotte's headed to the scaffold. Right now.

*Oh god. Blackout.*

## TWO.

*Lights on*
*The guillotine.*
*Marianne joins Olympe.*

OLYMPE. Oh god. OhGodOhGod, I can't watch this.

MARIANNE. You have to. If you don't capture it, they will. Write it down, Olympe.

OLYMPE. I can't, I do fiction, this is way too real.

MARIANNE. *That's why you need to write it.*

OLYMPE. I need to stay alive, and that's becoming harder and harder because of her. She's made them scared and they're taking it out on half of the human race. *Our half.* We have to get out of here now.

MARIANNE. I'm not leaving her, and neither are you.

OLYMPE. She doesn't need us now! All the sane people are leaving. Only the heartless wackos are left.

MARIANNE. And if you don't put the heart back in this revolution, *who will*? If you don't write this down, *who will*? *They* will. And that's how they win. And you don't want them to win. So stay right where you are, buck up, and witness this. That's what she deserves. What we all deserve. You said we're the heroes if you're writing it. So write.

*Olympe really wants to go—makes herself stay.*

OLYMPE. OK. Yes. OK. Scene: Charlotte Corday mounts the scaffold.

*Charlotte mounts the scaffold.*
*The crowd is rowdy.*
*She wears a white bonnet and dress.*

The red thing creaking as she stands tall against the grain. The crowd is rowdy this morning. They heave fat words at her, they bark. But she is not marred. The hem of her white dress flips in the wind like a ring of small fish at her feet.
I'm loving this narration, perhaps I should write novels.

MARIANNE. Focus please.

*Marianne and Olympe wave to Charlotte.*
*Charlotte delights when she sees them and waves back. Then goes back to her Steely Look of Unwavering Calm.*

OLYMPE. The young girl, a fair and beautiful creature in white, looks out towards the horizon, with posture braver and taller than any man gathered below the scaffold to watch her…die… Oh god. I can't. I can't. I'm sorry—

MARIANNE. Olympe, don't—

*But Olympe runs off—she can't take it.*
*Charlotte doesn't notice…but Marianne starts narrating to cover.*

Uh. So. The executioner yells: "Does the condemned have any last words?"

CHARLOTTE. Uh. Yes. I do…

MARIANNE. And. With confidence, and clarity, and a voice like a church bell ringing across the city—

CHARLOTTE. I KILLED ONE MAN, TO SAVE ONE HUNDRED THOUSAND.
VIVE LA REPUBLIC! VIVE LA FRANCE!
TELL MY FATHER I'M SORRY I DIDN'T GIVE HIM GRAND-CHILDREN.

*A sound of the guillotine, cheers, and a blackout cut her off…*

*Immediately a bright-white spot on Charlotte.*
*A moment alone with Charlotte…breathing…a moment suspended in this purgatory.*
*So so softly she sings…or her voice plays around her…*

*(Sung so softly, simply.)*
Who are we, without the riot?
What is a song, without a band?
What plays on, during the quiet?
Is the beat of the beat, and beat of the heart,
and the heart in our hand.

*Blackout on Charlotte.*
*Which gives way to…*

*Olympe in the corner of the city—breathing—scared.*
*That was too much to handle.*

*She's losing it. A gunshot or clamor in the distance startles her and sends her running off again.*

## THREE.

*Olympe's study. Marie holds a letter—wrapped in blue ribbon—she's stunned by it, scared of the letter, can't look away.*

*A sound of trumpets in the distance. Marie whips to the sound. Uh-oh.*

MARIE. Trumpets.

*Marianne runs in; she heard the trumpets too.*

MARIANNE. I heard them, they're coming for you, we have to—

*Marianne sees the letter Marie holds.*

What is that?

MARIE. It just arrived, and I—I think it's—

MARIANNE. No—

MARIE. I'm so sorry—

MARIANNE. Oh god.

| MARIE. | MARIANNE. |
|---|---|
| I'm so sorry, my friend, I'm so sorry. I'm so so sorry. | Oh god, oh god, oh god.<br>Oh god, oh god, oh god. |

*Marianne grasps the letter and falls on her knees. Vincent is dead. She knows this now.*

*Marie immediately cradles her, holds her, a true and great friend in this moment of terrible truths becoming known.*

MARIANNE. We worked so hard. And fought so hard. But right now. In this moment. I really don't know what I'd say if you asked me if I'd rather have the cause or have him here. In this moment? I might just toss all the revolutions for one more…anything.
Stride.

MARIE. Stand.

MARIANNE. Laugh.

MARIE. Spoon. Yes. But.
There is more to do, much more. Who will give your daughter her present if not her fearless, unbreakable mother?

*Marie reveals a beautiful little teacup with a big satin bow and a note.*

MARIANNE. *(Reading the note.)* "Teacup bows are the best. Love, Marie"

MARIE. They really are.

MARIANNE. Thank you.

MARIE. You're very welcome. And it will never be truly all right after losing him, but I'm going to say that it will because it's really nice to hear it sometimes. So. "It'll be all right. It'll be all right."

MARIANNE. *(Taking out her last letter to Vincent.)* I never… I never…sent my last letter. He never read it. He'll never—

MARIE. Read it now. To me. I'll hear it for him. What did you want to say?

*Marianne gets out the red-ribboned letter, reads from it—*

MARIANNE. I love you.

*Marianne folds a page and drops it.*

I love you.

*Marianne folds another page and drops it.*

I love you.

*A heavy KNOCK KNOCK KNOCK on the door.*

MARIE. Here we go.

MARIANNE. *No, not yet, don't leave, not yet.*

MARIE. I wish "yet" would listen.
But if we're honest we all knew this was coming.
What should I… Should I take a book? Or my play?
I'll give him your letter. And don't be sad for us. When you laugh? We will too.

*Marie smiles to Marianne, gathers all her ribbons…*
*The door creaks open—*

MARIANNE. It'll be all right.

MARIE. I think so.

*And Marie exits.*

*Marianne is alone for a moment.*
*She feels alone.*

*Then Olympe runs on.*

OLYMPE. Are they gone? Did they take her? Did they take anything of mine? Did they take the—

MARIANNE. I cannot talk to you right now.

OLYMPE. But she's gone though right? She's gone? She's—? *Oh god, where's my play? The new play? Did she take it?* Nonono, not that play. Not *that* play.

MARIANNE. How could you leave her, leave us all?

OLYMPE. *I will be with you in one minute but I think that Marie-Antoinette took my goddamn play.* Which means *they* have it now, which means…suddenly I wish I'd written a romantic comedy.

MARIANNE. *No one cares about your stupid play.*
Fiction doesn't matter if you're only using it to hide from reality—our reality—this reality, the one where your friends need you and are dying alone and you're trying to get your lines right.

OLYMPE. My… No. I'm trying to save our lives.

MARIANNE. There's nothing to save if you don't stand for anything.

OLYMPE. No, there's nothing to save if they kill us because they find my script in Marie-Antoinette's pocket. Now. *(A decision.)* Burn the pages. All my scripts, all the pamphlets. Anything left. We burn them, drown them, eat them, just get rid of them.

MARIANNE. No.

OLYMPE. Yes. We have to. And we leave tonight.

MARIANNE. No. No more of this running and dodging.

OLYMPE. If I don't, if they find any trace of my writing about any of us, they come for me, so start burning shit.

MARIANNE. And if you destroy them you destroy Charlotte and Marie and me. You destroy me. Because no one writes me down. But I thought you were. Sisterhood of heroes. Bullshit.

OLYMPE. Hey.

MARIANNE. NO. *(Talking about Vincent now.)* If you burn this story then everything we've fought for, everything that's happened, *every single person that has thrown their life into this will be as blank and mute as the paper you can't seem to fill.*

OLYMPE. You seem upset. I get that, but I'm just saying what we know is true: This fight isn't winnable any more. It's unstoppable this violence and—

MARIANNE. Isn't winnable?

OLYMPE. It's not.

MARIANNE. It is.

OLYMPE. It's not.

MARIANNE. *(Furious.) My husband died for this and you tell me that "this isn't winnable"?*

OLYMPE. Wait—what?

MARIANNE. *(Furious sarcasm.) It's just a game and he lost? NO. No—*

OLYMPE. *(She gets it.)* Marianne, wait—

MARIANNE. *It can be won, and it will be won, because people like him died for something real, unlike you and your goddamn stories that you abandon just when it's your time to stand for something.*

OLYMPE. I didn't—I'm sorry—

MARIANNE. They killed him like he was theirs to throw away as they pleased, but he was mine. *He was mine first.*

OLYMPE. Oh Marianne I'm—

MARIANNE. THIS IS NOT YOUR LINE.

OLYMPE. I'm sorry, I'm saying I'm sorry.

*Marianne is fucking furious.*

MARIANNE. You're always saying, saying, saying, and you never listen.
*Because this is all about you. Because you cannot feel anything unless it's staged.*
Well I'm gonna blow your mind here and tell you that this might not be *your* story in the end. Yes—Holy shit, the lady who has the

time to sit down and write her little skits *might not be the hero of the French Fucking Revolution.*

OLYMPE. *You came to me*, you all came to *me*, and asked for *my* help—

MARIANNE. *And you are failing us because you're not writing what's real.* The real world, the world you say you want to change, is too much to bear and you run. You run. You are allowed the privilege of telling stories, of naming yourself but here you tremble, afraid of your own power. Maybe that's why your writing *doesn't mean anything.*

OLYMPE. Doesn't mean anything?—I went to the National Assembly myself and—

MARIANNE. Told them what you thought they could handle. It didn't work. Now you're cowering in the shadows, abandoning your friends. Where is my pamphlet, my declaration, huh? You wrote half a play for *Marie-Antoinette because she's easy to stage. Where are my words, Olympe?* Or am I one of those breathless puppets to which you so often resort.

OLYMPE. You can't berate me and call me false and then beg me to help you.

MARIANNE. I'm not begging for anything from you. I don't need you.

OLYMPE. Finally! I've been waiting for you to declare *your damn self* and stop waiting for me.

MARIANNE. And I'm waiting for you to realize that you can't write the world if you're not in it! You can't change it if you can't see it! And you can't be a hero if you're too scared to show up. Or is this all just another drama you'll never finish?

*This chills Olympe.*

OLYMPE. At least I'm trying to create something. You're *just watching.*

MARIANNE. *Witnessing isn't just watching.*

OLYMPE. *And fear isn't weakness.* Fear is how you know you're paying attention.

MARIANNE. Maybe real revolution doesn't have time for either fiction or fear.

OLYMPE. *Because you don't think art matters.* You never did—*you never did.*

MARIANNE. Oh please—I have *always* stood by you.

*Throwing every bit of anger at Marianne with this—*

OLYMPE. You have *always* judged what I do, and doubted it, and mocked it and truly, in your honest heart, thought that *words don't work.* You would rather have twenty Charlottes in this fight than *one* sane artist because theatre seems to piss you off, but *death doesn't bother you.*

*Marianne smacks the papers out of Olympe's hands violently, like she's slapping a face.*
*Both Marianne and Olympe are shocked that she did.*
*Beat. Beat.*

MARIANNE. If your story is so easy to burn you won't need my help.

*Marianne leaves.*
*Olympe is alone…really alone now.*
*Freaking out.*

*Gathers her papers—will she burn them?*
*No. She can't. What does she do now?*
*Trying to conjure up a new character…*

OLYMPE. Perhaps a…new friend enters?

*Nothing.*

Or an old one?

*Across town trumpets announce…*

## FOUR.

*Marie, standing behind a rail, the ribbons fallen at her feet, defending herself at the Revolutionary Tribunal.*

MARIE. Marie enters.
This is not her usual crowd.

*Marianne enters, Olympe isn't here.*
*Charlotte, as Fraternité, in a mask presides.*

MARIANNE. The Trial of Marie-Antoinette. This is big. The world is watching. Even so the prosecutor knows that this is not a trial but a roast as he says:

CHARLOTTE/FRAT. "Prisoner 280, STATE YOUR DEFENSE."

MARIE. Well. I didn't do…it?

CHARLOTTE/FRAT. "The Tribunal accuses the former and immoral Austrian queen of crimes against humanity, morality, and the Republic. These crimes include: Being queen—"

MARIE. Oh, I *did* do that.

CHARLOTTE/FRAT. "Calling the former king a coward—"

MARIE. Definitely did that.

CHARLOTTE/FRAT. "Conspiring with the enemies of France to promote war and destroy the populace—"

MARIE. I did not do that—

CHARLOTTE/FRAT. "Orchestrating orgies at the palace—"

MARIE. No one told me about *that.*

CHARLOTTE/FRAT. "She sent French treasury money to her true homeland of Austria, designed the massacre of Swiss Guards, and—"

MARIE. Well this is *not* hilarious.

CHARLOTTE/FRAT. "And we're not done yet, folks. This woman is also accused of incestuous relations with her own son."

MARIE. NOW YOU LISTEN HERE. YOU MAY PUSH ME BUT DO NOT PUSH MY CHILDREN, NEVER MY CHILDREN, YOU DO NOT. SLANDER. CHILDREN. That accusation is a disgusting lie that *you* dreamt up, not me, which says a lot more about *the dreamer than it does the accused* you sick, pardon my American, DICKS.

MARIANNE. And the women in the room were taken with her passion, for how many of them had been accused of being bad mothers by strangers.

MARIE. You think you're making things better with this charade? But you're not, you're setting us all up for a—All I'm gonna say is watch out for ambitious little emperors whose names rhyme with *Shapoleon.*

MARIANNE. The prosecutor knew he risked losing the crowd so he got right to the point:

CHARLOTTE/FRAT. "The Tribunal has reached a decision."

MARIE. YOU CAME IN HERE WITH A DECISION.

CHARLOTTE/FRAT. "Prisoner 280, Marie-Antoinette, otherwise known as the Former Queen of France and Navarre, otherwise known as the Bitch, Madame Deficit, the Widow Capet, and the Soon-To-Be-No-More.
You are condemned and sentenced to die by the guillotine. *Now.*"

MARIE. *(Summoning up her deepest, most regal power for this laser-like take-down of her enemy.)* Then you, sirs, bear not the marks of men, but the instincts of animals. And with your mouth of hate and hands of hair, you rip not your enemies in half but your country, *your country is gored on your watch*—so you, Followers of Animal Order, will remove the squint from your eyes so that you may fully see with whom you are dealing. Do you see? Do you see this woman, this mother, this citizen queen, do you See. Me. Now?
You do. And now we are linked. And now, like a simple song played on and on, you will never. forget. me.
Proceed.

*A quick shift to a guillotine.*
*Marie's wig is suddenly gone, her hair is short and messy.*
*Olympe finally shows up…terrified to be there, to witness.*

OLYMPE. They cut her hair.

*Marianne hears this, sees that Olympe is there.*

She aged a decade in a moment. To her, she *was still* France. And today, France was losing its head in a dirty gown. But she doesn't betray herself. She doesn't weep. She acts every bit the royalty.

MARIANNE. Then the wind drops

OLYMPE. The world hums to a hush.

MARIANNE. And the world begins to never forget.

*Marie looks to Marianne and Olympe*
*who nod and smile supportively.*

MARIE. *(Quick and quiet.)* Marie enters. Is she late? Or lost? What were they talking about? Was it her? It's always her. Or is she being her again? It's a confusing time. Hello. Marie.

CHARLOTTE/FRAT. Does the condemned have any last words…

MARIE. Yes.
I…

*She accidentally steps on Frat's foot.*

*(To him.)* I'm so sorry, I didn't mean to—

*A sound of the guillotine,*
*Marie reveals and drops one red ribbon.*
*Cheers and a blackout cut her off.*

*Immediately a bright white spot*
*on Marie suspended in whatever purgatory this is.*
*She sings, so softly, so simply…*

Who are we, without our power?
What's a truth, none understand?
Fame's a force, building era from hour,
and the beat of the beat, and the beat of the heart,
and heart in our hand.

*Marie breathes, mourns, breathes, then looks right out at us before…*

*Blackout on Marie.*

## FIVE.

*Olympe in her study.*
*After seeing Marie's execution she's disgusted, horrified, scared as hell.*
*Papers everywhere, scripts, pamphlets.*
*She hates hates HATES them all.*
*Olympe throws the papers, scatters them, hurls them.*

OLYMPE. WHY DON'T YOU WORK?!
Air and ink and make believe and nothing is working and nothing is helping and nothing that I'm doing is real. *An entire life of nothing that's real.*

*Marianne enters…*

MARIANNE. That's not completely true.

*Olympe swings around to see her friend—a rush of feeling.*

OLYMPE. *Marianne*, you're here, oh my god, I'm so sorry. You're right. What am I doing with all this? What's the point, what's real? I don't even know anymore.

MARIANNE. You showed up for Marie. *That's* the point, that's real.

OLYMPE. I know I let you down. I'm not brave like you, I'm just… loquacious. A fact that's probably going to get me killed.

MARIANNE. You're not at the end yet. You're stronger than you think, and your words do matter. They are braver than you are. Let them loose and they'll outlast you. That's what I think. And…I'm sorry too.

*Does Olympe hug her here? Need her, grip her hand, something.*

And you'll be happy to know that you were right.

OLYMPE. Oh. About what?

MARIANNE. I am better at this than you. I wrote my own pamphlet, which was so good it became a declaration.

*Clears her throat. The declaration from memory:*

"We, the free and proud women and men of Saint-Domingue, deny the unjust power of France and her agents of torture and greed. The sun of this island shines on an independent nation of liberty, not property."

OLYMPE. Not. Bad. Citizen.

MARIANNE. Oh ya know. Writing what I want.

OLYMPE. What we want…

MARIANNE. You know what I really want? I want people to live their lives and make babies and eat too much and do experimental theatre.

OLYMPE. Now there's a France I can believe in.

MARIANNE. And let's be kind, shall we. In honor of Vincent, and Charlotte, and crazy ass Marie-Antoinette, let us *laugh too loudly and too often*, and call out the hypocrites of our age until they are the butt of the joke. That's what we give our children. A good laugh.

OLYMPE. My son. All grown up with a son of his own. What will he think of me?

MARIANNE. He'll think his mom doesn't take any shit from anyone, says what she believes, and is willing to die for it.

OLYMPE. But—yes—but I don't particularly *want* to die for this. I would rather live for it.

MARIANNE. Uh. Yeah. I think the real win is changing the world and living to enjoy it.

OLYMPE. Right? This stuff is scary as hell.

MARIANNE. This is the "Reign of *Terror*" not the "Reign of Agree to Disagree."

OLYMPE. *OK*, I was trying to be brave because you were, but goddammit I want to outlive these fuckers.

MARIANNE. Me too!

OLYMPE. Let's just skip to the part when we're all over this bullshit and we can tell our grandchildren how we beat these idiots.

MARIANNE. Beat them black and goddamn blue.

OLYMPE. With our drama!

MARIANNE. And our sashes!

OLYMPE. And our fists goddammit I want to punch those assholes in their eye sockets!
*(To those assholes.)* You want a revolution? COME AT ME.

MARIANNE. COME AT ME TOO.

OLYMPE. OK, come at her first and then me.

*They share a much-needed smile.*

MARIANNE. OK. One of us has to survive this. Whoever does will have a lot of work to do. And three really chatty ghosts making sure they do it.

OLYMPE. I think it'll be you.

MARIANNE. I think it'll be you.

*Marianne hands Olympe a pen.*

Either way. *We're* the heroes. If you're writing the story.

OLYMPE. I should probably hurry up then.

*Olympe smiles. Grabs the pen to write...*

*KNOCK KNOCK KNOCK at her door.*
*Marianne holds her hand and she:*

The Trial of…
Me.

*BANG BANG BANG of a gavel.*
*As a swift surge into…*
"The Trial of Olympe de Gouges"

## SIX.

*A podium swings in front of Olympe. Charlotte and Marie, as Fraternités in masks, enter. Olympe is surrounded, arguing for her life on all sides.*

CHARLOTTE/FRAT. BY THE AUTHORITY OF THE COMMITTEE FOR PUBLIC SAFETY, YOU ARE HEREBY TRIED WITH TREASON FOR CONSISTENT AND AGGRESSIVE THEATRICAL ACTIONS.

OLYMPE. OK. So. The thing about that is…

*Will she deny it or not? Not. She takes a stand.*

Yes. Yes. If being a traitor is loving my country enough to shame it for being less than its best self, then I am one, yes I am, and god knows I don't do anything less than aggressive theatre.

*One of the Frats reveals Olympe's play—a threat to her.*

CHARLOTTE/FRAT. Your play is a treasonous tract,

CHARLOTTE/FRAT and MARIE/FRAT. a shameful drama, poorly penned—

OLYMPE. First draft, Jesus.

CHARLOTTE/FRAT. maliciously and purposefully composed to attack the sovereignty of the people.

OLYMPE. I would never attack the sovereignty—

MARIE/FRAT. Your play depicts the former queen, does it not?

OLYMPE. Well yes but not in a fine light.

CHARLOTTE/FRAT. You portray that woman as a sympathetic figure for all to see.

OLYMPE. Nonono, the whole point is that the queen learns a lesson. A lesson about the true north of the Republic.

MARIE/FRAT. And she learns this lesson in your play?

OLYMPE. Yes.

MARIE/FRAT. So she's capable of learning?

OLYMPE. Yes.

CHARLOTTE/FRAT. Which makes her a sympathetic figure.

OLYMPE. *It just makes her human. I'm* the sympathetic figure in the play. And *I'm* the one that convinces her that democracy is better than royalty. That character is Olympe de Gouges SO AS NOT TO BE CONFUSED WITH ANYONE ELSE BUT ME. This play proves I'm a patriot. And anyway, I haven't even gotten to the end of it.

MARIE/FRAT. What happens at the end?

OLYMPE. *(Making this up—deliberate* Les Mis *references.)* Uh… we'll probably…hear the people sing? And the sound of distant drums?

MARIE/FRAT. It's a musical?

OLYMPE. For the whole family. You'll laugh, you'll cry, there's a barricade.

CHARLOTTE/FRAT. By unanimous decision, this Tribunal states that Olympe de Gouges, the female playwright—

OLYMPE. Just *playwright.*

CHARLOTTE/FRAT. —is guilty and shall be punished by death—

OLYMPE. You can't kill me for this, I work in the theatre, it's a nonprofit.

CHARLOTTE/FRAT and MARIE/FRAT. We kill a lot of people, Miss De Gouges.

OLYMPE. No. You *can't* kill me. I'm pregnant.

*Pause.*

CHARLOTTE/FRAT and MARIE/FRAT. The Tribunal does not think you're pregnant.

OLYMPE. But I am. Definitely pregnant.

CHARLOTTE/FRAT and MARIE/FRAT. We're pretty sure that you're not.

OLYMPE. Gimme a few weeks.

CHARLOTTE/FRAT. The condemned shall be killed tomorrow morning and justice will hereby be served.

OLYMPE. THIS IS NOT JUSTICE. You say you fight for freedom and equality but that means art and ideas which is my life's work. A work *in progress* you might note.
I mean you can't kill the writers, that's Democracy 101.
*I* AM NOT THE PROBLEM, *YOU* ARE THE PROBLEM.

CHARLOTTE/FRAT and MARIE/FRAT. The Tribunal does not think we're the problem.

OLYMPE. *Goddammit—come on—no—NO—YOU GUYS? YOU GUYS ARE FUCKING UP THE REVOLUTION.*

*Swift transition as the world around her empties, vanishes, leaving—*

## SEVEN.

*Olympe.*
*Alone.*

OLYMPE. Not like this. No. No, it's not ending like this. *I'm not ending like this.*

*Trying to tear out the stage curtains, the floorboards, her costume. How does she stop this play?!*

THIS IS NOT. *THE END.*

*She stops, realizes.*

You don't write what you know, you write what you *want*. OK. *(Trying to narrate her way out of this.)* Olympe de Gouges. 38, very well liked and respected in her field and all the politicians and revolutionaries and theatre critics think she's great, and she will live a long time, and eat as many macarons as she can carry, and she will make it out of this, and she is just walking home from rehearsal, and enjoying Paris in the fall and—

*Charlotte appears.*

CHARLOTTE. You know that's not as good a story.

OLYMPE. I don't care if it is.

CHARLOTTE. Yeah you do. I know you do.

OLYMPE. No, THIS IS MY LIFE, NOT A PLAY. A PLAY YOU CAN WALK OUT OF.

*Marie appears, only ever repeats her last words.*

MARIE. I'm so sorry, I didn't mean to—

OLYMPE. Marie—help—*ribbons.*

MARIE. I'm so sorry, I didn't mean to—

OLYMPE. What is she saying?

CHARLOTTE. Her last words. I think that's all she remembers—

MARIE. I'm so sorry, I didn't mean to—

CHARLOTTE. Do you have your last words worked out yet?

OLYMPE. NO NO I DON'T.

CHARLOTTE. You should think about it, writer.

OLYMPE. *I am not this kind of writer!*

*Marianne enters.*

MARIANNE. What kind of writer are you?

OLYMPE. The *really scared kind.*

CHARLOTTE. Scared that you didn't matter?

MARIANNE. *(Re: Marie.)* Or that she's going to be more famous than all of us.

MARIE. I'm so sorry, I didn't mean to—

OLYMPE. No No *NO.* I'm scared of…of ending.

MARIANNE. Then don't. Turn the end into a beginning.

CHARLOTTE. *(A bad idea.)* A play that doesn't end? Oh god.

OLYMPE. *(A great idea.)* A play that doesn't end? Oh god!

MARIANNE. You're writing what you want, right? So defy them with your story. They can't touch the play in your mind.

OLYMPE. The play in my mind?

MARIANNE. Yeah. Play that one.

OLYMPE. But. I need *real help here*, not fiction.

MARIANNE. It might be fiction, but it's not fake.
The beating hearts in front of you are real.
The gathering of people is real.
The time we spend together, this time, is real.
The story is real when it starts.

*The lights rise slowly on the real audience.*

OLYMPE. Has it? Started? But it can't write itself.

MARIANNE. Oh girl. It already is.

*Olympe starts to see the audience around her.*

Your story isn't yours now.

MARIE. I'm so sorry, I didn't mean to—

OLYMPE. But…whose is it?

CHARLOTTE. *(Pointing to the audience.)* I think…theirs.

*Olympe sees the audience. Is amazed. Have they been there the whole time?*

OLYMPE. But…who are…who…?

MARIANNE. I don't know. But they showed up and seem to be listening.

OLYMPE. Are they armed?

CHARLOTTE. I think they're just…interested.

MARIANNE. Which is what you wanted, isn't it? An audience.

CHARLOTTE. A message.

MARIANNE. A story of our own.

*Marie giggles softly.*

OLYMPE. Yes. *(Absolutely overwhelmed by this.)* What a thing.

*What does she say to a live audience? Tearfully but proud. To us…*

Thank you. For your time. For listening. Thank you.
It's an honor to…stand before you and—

*As she stands before us…*

*The world around her changes…*
*To the scaffold. We become the mob.*

*Exactly as we heard in the prologue…*
*Anticipation. Wood creaking.*
*And the sound of a scared breath—Olympe's breath—*
*Except it's everywhere, it's our breath, it's history's breath.*
*Breath—Breath—*

To stand before you and—

*Charlotte and Marie start singing "Our Song."*

This whole time…I've been standing…before you and—

*A sharp white light on, or the engorging shadow of…*
*A guillotine, its blade rising to the top.*

That's not a way to start a comedy.

MARIANNE. I don't know about you, but when good stories end I always want to go right back to beginning.

*Olympe hears this, understands, grips Marianne's hand. She concentrates, conjuring up the ending to her story exactly as she would have it go.*

OLYMPE. The death of Olympe de Gouges.

*Marianne narrates for her…*

MARIANNE. A bright fall day, four P.M., light lingering on the trees and slanting low on the Place de la Révolution. Olympe de Gouges walks up the wooden steps onto the sturdy stage. Yes, she thinks, a stage.

OLYMPE. A stage…

MARIANNE. She thinks of Marie-Antoinette, who was on this very spot only weeks ago.

OLYMPE. Marie.

MARIANNE. She thinks of Charlotte Corday—

OLYMPE. Charlotte…

MARIANNE. and the wildness of her hands and heart, also here not long ago.

OLYMPE. All of us.

CHARLOTTE. She also thinks of a woman she passed in the streets a few weeks ago who held her head high and wore a red sash that said "Revolution For All." To Olympe she looked like the symbol of freedom.

OLYMPE. *La Marianne.*

MARIANNE. *(Sung.)*
Who are we, without a story?
Lost at sea, in search of land…

CHARLOTTE. That woman hummed a soft song that slipped into Olympe's ear that day.

MARIANNE. *(Sung.)*
We survive the roughness of glory

CHARLOTTE. A song sticks.

MARIANNE. *(Sung.)*
By passing the beat of the beat of the heart
From hand to hand.

*Marie and/or Charlotte continues humming the song.*

OLYMPE. A simple song played on and on.

CHARLOTTE. And on and on.

MARIANNE. Now Olympe never actually met these women, but on the scaffold in that moment—

OLYMPE. Her moment.

MARIANNE. She writes what she wants: her own story.

OLYMPE. *Her own story.*

MARIANNE. And her story is one of…sisters.

CHARLOTTE. Sisters know what you mean when you don't have the words.

MARIANNE. So she tells herself a story as she looks out on the masses of people.

OLYMPE. Yes. She finds herself with an…audience. And a monologue. This she can handle.
So she quiets that fiction in her mind.

*Charlotte and Marie stop humming "Our Song"…*

And she summons up her truest self.

And the time is now.
And the stage is set.

MARIANNE. "Does the condemned have any last words."

OLYMPE. And she knows that a story is more alive than a fact. A story is what lives.
Olympe de Gouges stands before them
And she is good.
And she is not alone.
And with her last moments, she calls out like a queen, like a righteous girl, like a mother of nations, she calls out:
"Children of France. Avenge my death."

MARIANNE. Which wasn't exactly what she meant. She really meant:

OLYMPE. "Please do my plays after I'm gone."

MARIANNE. Or:

OLYMPE. "Don't settle for the story that they're giving you."

MARIANNE. or maybe she just meant:

OLYMPE. "May God Have No Pity, You Motherfuckers."

CHARLOTTE. That's my girl.

MARIANNE. But the crowd understood her.

OLYMPE. And a downpour of applause rained on Olympe like the curtain call she'd always wanted.

MARIANNE. Which surprised the executioner so much that he held the blade longer than he'd ever done before. And that pause cracked him right down the center. And in that crack grew a rustle, that turned into a rumble, that turned into a…

*Marie giggles.*

CHARLOTTE. The executioner *laughed*. Not at her, at himself. He caught a glimpse of his own hypocrisy. Which was horribly, terribly funny.

OLYMPE. And the vindication of Olympe de Gouges started, as it should, with a joke.

CHARLOTTE. And a song was sung that Olympe could only hear—

OLYMPE. That Olympe could hear only—

*Marianne sings to Olympe…*

MARIANNE. *(Sung.)*
Who are we, without a story?

OLYMPE. As the blade fell.

*Olympe takes a slow, proud, grand bow thanking her audience for listening. At the nadir of the bow—*

*The sound of the guillotine.*

*But Olympe stands tall again to tell us…*

OLYMPE. And a story…begins.

*Blackout.*

**End of Play**

## PROPERTY LIST

*(Use this space to create props lists for your production)*

## SOUND EFFECTS

*(Use this space to create sound effects lists for your production)*

## Note on Songs/Recordings, Images, or Other Production Design Elements

## NOTES

*(Use this space to make notes for your production)*

# NOTES

*(Use this space to make notes for your production)*

## NOTES

*(Use this space to make notes for your production)*

## NOTES

*(Use this space to make notes for your production)*

# NOTES

*(Use this space to make notes for your production)*

## NOTES

*(Use this space to make notes for your production)*